FOREX TRADING

The Complete Series

Part 1: Two round number strategies

Part 2: Two strategies with weekly pivots

Part 3: Trading with the Weekly High and Low

Part 4: Trade several strategies simultaneously

Heikin Ashi Trader

Splendid Island

Ormidia, Larnaca

Table of Contents

PART 1:
TWO ROUND NUMBER
STRATEGIES

Introduction

Anyone who can trade the futures like the E-mini or NQ will be successful in the forex markets, as I always thought. After all, human behavior remains the same at all times and in all financial markets. All you have to do is study it, so that you can develop trading strategies that are universally applicable.

If this statement is correct in principle, it is equally true that every market has its own characteristics. Traders who trade the same market for years are aware of this. The same patterns occur repeatedly. Their market prepares trends in a specific way. The experienced trader knows (or feels) when to get in or when to stay away.

If these things also apply to the forex markets to a certain extent, then undoubtedly they have their own peculiarities, which only apply to them. Forex markets are not really markets, because there is no place or central instance where buyers and sellers meet. Unlike stock markets and commodities, there is no central entity where forex pairs are traded.

The foreign exchange market "works" thanks to a network of commercial banks that communicate with each other and with their major customers. This was previously, and still is done over the phone, though the internet and today's infrastructure have largely replaced that type of communication.

However, this decentralized structure ensures that an unlimited number of market players are able to participate in the transactions. There are actually enough traders at any time who are willing to buy or sell this currency or that, at this price or that. As a result, foreign exchange trading is a very efficient trading activity. In other words, there are few or hardly any inefficiencies a trader could exploit, as is the case in the much less efficient penny stock markets, for example. Those who like to exploit inefficiencies are better off in these markets than they are in the forex. The order book (if you could even speak of such a thing in forex) is incredibly deep. No market is more liquid than the forex.

It is widely known that more than USD 4 trillion is being transacted on the international currency markets on each trading day. This number varies, but it has been constant for years. Of course, most of those transactions take place in the so-called "majors", the main pairs. The best known among them are EURUSD, USDCHF, GBPUSD and USDJPY.

So if these markets are very liquid, and millions of traders trade in them worldwide, this also explains the fact that the fluctuations here are limited. You will rarely find a day when, for example, the EURUSD has risen or fallen more than 1%. As a rule, the fluctuation range is much lower. Of course, this has consequences for the nature of these markets. Trend behavior, such as that found in commodities or equities, is more the exception than the rule. Currency markets mainly move sideways on most trading days.

So, if you trade strategies that are based on trend behavior (such as trend following strategies), you are not going to do very well in those markets. It would be much better if a trend trader would trade some stocks from the Nasdaq, like Apple, Amazon or Facebook.

And thus, apart from the decentralized structure of the foreign exchange markets, we find their second important feature: <u>foreign exchange markets tend to show trend behavior in exceptional cases.</u> In other words, currency pairs run sideways on most trading days. If you tend not believe that, then look at this EURUSD chart (Image 1). No one can argue with the fact that the pair shows a clear downward trend in this period. In other words, you see a clearly visible downward movement in the chart.

Image 1: EURUSD, daily chart, June - December 2014

Does this not contradict what I have just said about the currency markets? By no means, because if you look closely, you will find that, although the market was "generally" in a downtrend mode, it still ran sideways on most trading days (yellow blocks in the chart). The downward movement comes, as it were in spurts, and usually unexpectedly. The question I have is: will you be in the right position when the next downward push occurs?

I think the answer is probably clear. Most market players have either no position or even the wrong position the moment this happens.

In other words, it is very difficult to be successful with trend following strategies in the currency markets. Either you need a lot of patience (in some phases of the downtrend shown above, the EURUSD went sideways for thirty days!), or, you are an investor who does not look at daily charts.

However, if you are a trader and you want to make money trading forex pairs, you'll have a hard time succeeding if you bet on trends.

And there is more. Because of the historically unique situation, we have been experiencing an interest rate environment for years, where you could almost speak of the abolition of interest. This is particularly the case in the euro area (as of July 2019), where the ECB has artificially set interest rates at 0 for years. What do you think this means for foreign exchange trading, which is known to be determined by the interest rate of the respective country (or the currency area as in the euro zone)? This of course means that volatility is almost non existent. Look at this table of historical volatility in the EURUSD, then you understand what I am saying.

Image 2: EUR/USD daily volatility

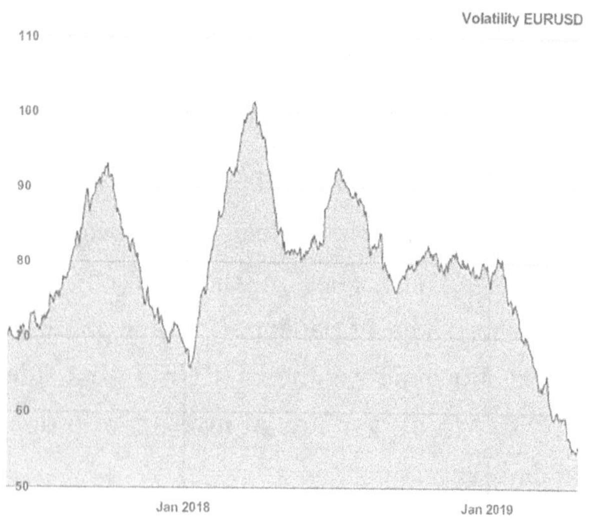

So, if at the beginning of 2018, there was still a good daily fluctuation of 100 pips in the EUR/USD, this was only 52 pips a year later. This means that, as a trader you can expect a maximum daily fluctuation of 52 pips in this currency pair. Note: Maximum fluctuation. So we are measuring from the high to the low of the day, and no trader in the world is known to be able to trade the high and low of the day and make a profit out of it. If there is any profit, then of course this would be less than 52 pips.

This means that the world's largest currency pair moves less than 0.5% per trading day.

So, you should ask yourself if it is worth trading on such a market if there is hardly any movement.

Let's summarize. The foreign exchange market is currently (as of July 2019) characterized by 3 special features:

1. High liquidity
2. Daily fluctuations mostly below 1%
3. Historically low volatility

If you look at these three facts, it becomes clear to the reader that any trader approaching this market with traditional trading techniques is likely to have a hard time succeeding.

It follows that forex trading works best with such strategies that take the above-mentioned peculiarities into account. There may be exceptions to this rule (the financial crisis 2008 and the euro crisis 2012 were such exceptions). However, the above specifics apply 80% of the time. A forex trader is therefore good at taking them seriously and taking them into consideration when choosing which strategy/strategies to use.

That's why I came up with the idea of introducing some tried-and-tested strategies that accurately reflect these peculiarities. These strategies are easy to understand and implement. There is one prerequisite – that certain phenomena and patterns occur again and again in forex, and traders try to make a profit out of this.

Strategy 1:
The round number strategy

Those who study charts of currency pairs will find that the market often turns on the so-called "round number" and temporarily starts to run in the other direction again. By "round number" I mean for example 1.1200 in EURUSD or 0.9800 in USDCHF or 1.3200 in USDCAD.

Of course, I do not claim that the market always turns once this round number is reached, that is, as soon as, for example, the EURUSD has reached 1.1200 or 1.1100. Nevertheless, I have observed that there are more buy or sell orders around these round numbers, which all have to be executed as soon as the EURUSD reaches this level. And of course this has consequences for the price trend. The first strategy tries to capitalize on this fact by assuming the "likelihood" that the market will turn, at least temporarily.

Image 3: USDCAD, hourly chart

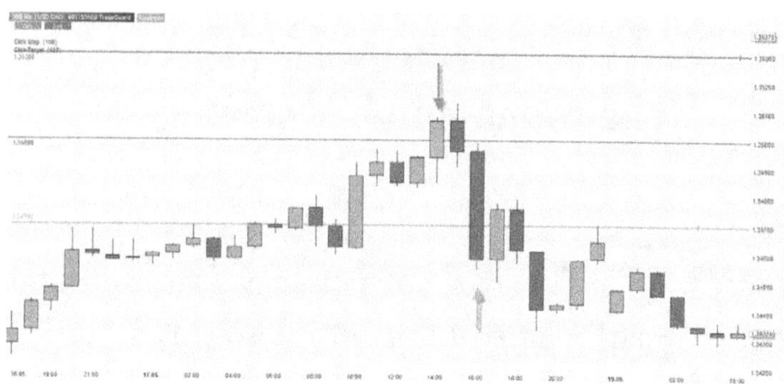

Image 3 shows an example of how this simple strategy works. The middle line represents the level of the round number. At the time of the screenshot, it was 1.3500 in the currency pair USDCAD. In this case, the trader places a limit sell order exactly at 1.3500 (red arrow above) with a stop loss of 30 pips, i.e. 1.3530. The red horizontal line at the top shows the stop loss level. The price target is 30 pips lower and waits for 1.3470 (green horizontal line below) to be reached. The market reached this price target after two hours (green arrow below). As you can see, this was done without hitting the stop loss order at 1.3530.

Accordingly, the trader creates a "playing field" of a total of 60 pips. Thirty pips risk and thirty pips chance. Thus, he works with a risk reward ratio of 1:1. He risks 30 pips to win exactly 30 pips. If he is right in 50% of the cases, he will win as many pips as he loses. So he has to achieve a hit rate of over 50% in order to trade profitably. To illustrate this, let's look at a few examples where the trader made several "round number" trades.

Image 4: USDCAD, 4-hour chart

In this example, the trader made a total of 14 trades. The green arrows symbolize "winning trades" the red "losing trades." There were 10 long trades and 4 short trades. The pair was in a sideways movement at this stage, which was approximately between 1.3400 and 1.3300 (between the inner blue horizontal lines). As you can see, most of the time the pair turned around the round number. Ten of fourteen trades ended in a profit. This results in the following performance:

Profitable trades: 10 x 30 pips = 300 pips
Loss Trades: 4 x 30 pips   = -120 pips

Total: **180 pips**

The trader was thus able to generate a result of 180 pips in this period. This corresponds to a hit rate of 71.43%, which is of course excellent. But you should not forget that he works with a risk reward ratio of 1:1. So he has to reach a hit rate that is higher than 50% in order to trade profitably.

In the following example, we can see that this is not always so easy.

Image 5: USD/CHF, 4-hour chart

In this example, the trader traded in the USD/CHF (US Dollar - Swiss Francs) currency pair. The pair traded between 1.0000 and 0.9900 during this period. In other words, the pair moved around the so-called parity (1 to 1), meaning that you got exactly one Swiss franc for one dollar.

The pair touched the "round number" seven times during this period. The trader was able to carry out 7 trades. However, he was not as successful here as in the USDCAD. He was able to complete four trades, with a gain and three with a loss. The trader achieved the following result:

Profitable trades: 4 x 30 pips   = 120 pips

Loss Trades: 3 x 30 pips   = -90 pips

Total: **30 pips**

As you can see, the trader had to "work" a lot more to make a profit, but it was a profit, nevertheless. Four winning trades on seven equals a hit rate of 57.14%. This second example shows a more realistic assessment of this strategy. This may seem like a disappointment or a weakness to some beginners, but in my experience, these are still excellent results, of which a trader can live very well.

Let's assume the trader chooses this strategy. He does an average of 20 trades a month and his hit rate settles at around 60%. He achieves the following monthly result:

Profitable trades: 12 x 30 pips = 360 pips
Loss trades: 8 x 30 pips   = -240 pips
Total: **120 pips**

In that case, the trader would realize an average profit of 120 pips per month. This may seem "disappointing" to some, especially if one starts from the very optimistic assumption that, with day trading or scalping in the forex market, you could realize 50 pips a day. I can tell you from experience that only very few traders (if any) achieve that.

But having a robust monthly yield of 120 pips is quite feasible for any trader using this strategy. Incidentally, it depends on the position size – what 120 pips means for you in dollars. If you trade with a so called mini lot (USD 10,000), you will not get rich with a result of USD 120 a month. But if you trade a standard lot (USD 100,000), then you might make USD 1,200 per month.

However, if you are in a position to achieve this result on a regular basis, you really have all the doors open for a successful trading career. You can then either work your way up with your own trading capital and soon, you might be able to trade two or three standard lots. Or you could put your skills at the disposal of investors from all over the world who would like to "capitalize" your trading account. You could then start to trade with much higher positions.

In this way, you are more likely to earn an income that exceeds USD 10,000 per month. I explained how to do this in my book: "How to start a trading business with USD 500".

The round-figure strategy works well with the following currency pairs: USDCAD, USDCHF, AUDUSD, NZDUSD, EURJPY, USDJPY, EURGBP and EURCHF

I would rather avoid the better known EURUSD and GBPUSD pairs with this strategy. You will achieve below-average results here with the 30 pips strategy. A lot of traders worldwide trade these two pairs, making the chances of being profitable very low.

The strategy is a pure "set and forget strategy". This means that you should always work with bracket orders. Set a limit buy or sell order on the round number, depending on whether you want to go long or short. At the same time, your order activates a price target of 30 pips and a stop loss order of 30 pips. Once the trade is in the market, you can turn off the computer, because it is the market that decides whether the price target or the stop will be reached first.

So you can trade this strategy even if you still have a day job. You can do this by setting your limits in the morning in the currency pairs in which you want to trade. Thanks to the bracket orders, you do not need to babysit the trades.

Strategy 2:
The Stop Hunting Strategy

The second strategy is a simple "momentum strategy", based on the assumption that the big players in the foreign exchange market like to "chase" stops at the round number. Although everyone knows that you should not place your stop at the round number, many stop orders are still being put at this level, mostly by institutional market participants.

The idea of this strategy is precisely that you can assume that, as soon as the market approaches the round number, momentum traders will "hunt" the round number (and the stops waiting there). The strategy assumes that if the market is only 15 pips away from the round number, it will usually get the round number. The next Image illustrates this strategy.

Image 6: USDCAD, 15-minute chart

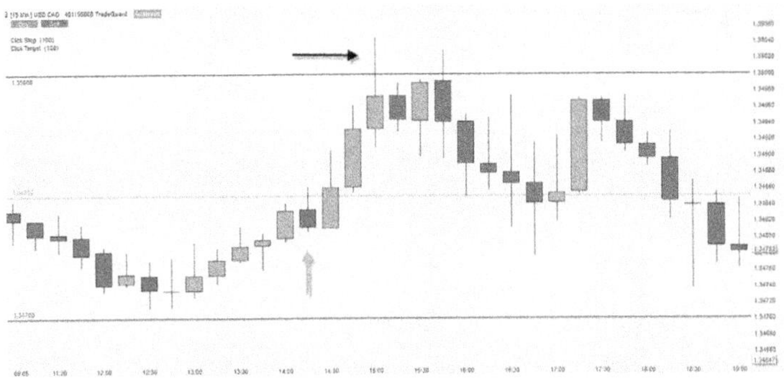

In this example, in the currency pair **USDCAD**, the market approached the round number 1.3500. As soon as this happens the trader places a stop-buy order at 1.3485, i.e. 15 pips below the round number (green arrow below). As you can see, the market reached the price target (top horizontal line and arrow) after four candles. The bottom red horizontal line shows the stop loss level, which was 15 pips below the entry, i.e. 1.3470.

The trader tries to profit from the expected "run" on the round number. The last 15 pips, so to speak. He is willing to take 15 pips of risk because he assumes that the likelihood is higher that the round number will be touched before the market falls behind.

Again, the trader works with a risk reward ratio of 1: 1. He risks 15 pips to win 15 pips. This strategy is easy to implement with bracket orders. If the trader leaves his trading desk after the entry, he can return after an hour to determine the realized gain of 15 pips.

Image 7: USDCAD, hourly chart

In this example, the trader made five trades with this strategy, of which three were winning trades (green arrows) and two were losing trades (red arrows). Overall, the trader went four times long just before the 1.3500 mark and once short just before the 1.3400 mark. The 15 pips profit target and the 15 pips stop-loss distance frame the "playing field" of this simple strategy.

Again, the trader should also expect loss trades to occur regularly. As always in trading, it depends on the ratio of profit and loss trades, which hopefully will be decided to the advantage of the trader. In the example in Image 7 we had the following result:

Profitable trades: 3 x 15 pips = 45 pips

Loss trades: 2 x 15 pips   = -30 pips

Total: **15 pips**

As you can see, the result of this strategy seems modest at first glance, but this 60% hit rate appears achievable to me, with some practice. Also with this strategy,

I would avoid the two pairs EURUSD and GBPUSD and concentrate on the above list of Strategy 1. Interestingly enough, most newbies trade EURUSD and **GBPUSD**, although these are proven to be the pairs the hardest to trade.

Consider forex trading like a probability game

Of course, variants of these two strategies are feasible and there are traders who trade the two strategies with slightly modified parameters. Before you change the parameters in the strategies I have presented here, you should first test the modifications for a while before going live.

Forex trading is a very different game than trading stocks or futures. You should therefore approach the matter with the right (market-adjusted) strategies. As I said in the beginning, in my opinion "range strategies", which rely on a quick take-off of a few pips, are the best in forex, due to the three above mentioned characteristics of this market.

The two strategies are good examples of how to gradually build a trading business, based on calculated probabilities. Since the patterns in forex trading repeat themselves over and over again, you can approach the matter with very simple methods and let the math work for you in the long term. As you know, you only need to make a little more profit than loss to earn a fortune in forex. That's why I think it's better to approach things systematically. The two strategies presented here are a first step in this direction.

PART 2:
TWO STRATEGIES WITH WEEKLY PIVOTS

How to trade the weekly Pivots

Just as in the two strategies with the round number (Part 1 of this series), I would like to present two strategies with "weekly pivots". If you are not familiar with the concept of pivots, I will briefly explain what they mean.

Pivot points, or simply "pivots", were originally developed by floor traders in the commodity markets, in order to determine potential turning points. A distinction is made between the pivot itself, and three resist and three support levels. The pivot is the pivotal point of the trading day. It is the average of the high, low and close prices of the previous trading day. If the forex pair is trading above the pivot, this generally indicates a bullish sentiment. Conversely, if the pair is trading below the pivot, pivot traders are bearish and are more likely to take short positions.

The three support and resistance levels, which are also calculated on the basis of the previous trading day, are also important. They serve the pivot trader as possible entry levels for trades, or as potential price targets.

Just as you can calculate pivot points on a daily basis, you can also calculate them on a weekly, or even on a monthly basis. Most trading platforms have already implemented them automatically. It takes a few clicks to install them on a chart.

Image 1: USDJPY,
4-hour chart, weekly pivots, 09.30.to 10.04.2019

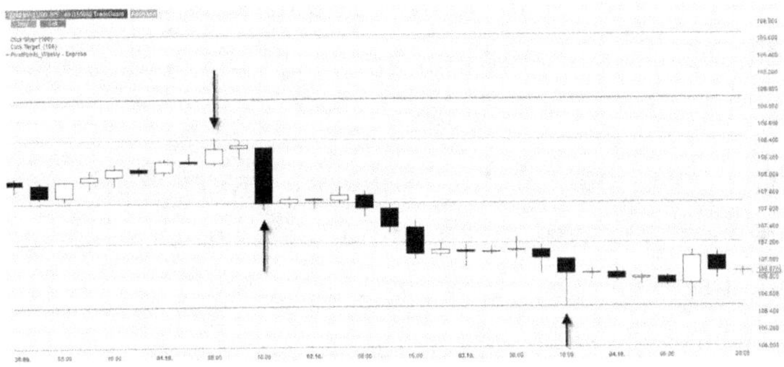

Image 1 shows the weekly pivots for the week from September 30 to October 4, 2019 in the USDJPY pair. The seven horizontal lines were automatically calculated by my broker platform, based on the closing data from the previous week. The middle line is the pivot itself. Above it, you can see the three resistances R1, R2 and R3. Below are the three support levels S1, S2 and S3.

As you can see, USDJPY first traded in the direction of the R1 level, and reached it quite accurately at around noon on October 1. It then dropped back to the weekly pivot in the afternoon. The next day, USDJPY was trading under the pivot and reached S1 in the afternoon and then dropped below that level. In the afternoon of October 3, USDJPY reached the S2 level.

Apart from the touch with S1 on October 2, the market turned pretty much exactly at each pivot level. Sometimes this happens exactly on a pip. Needless to say, as a trader you can take advantage of that.

The idea of the two pivot strategies I present here are similar to the round number strategies. I have simply adapted them to the concept of pivots. The weekly pivots, not the daily pivots!

Before we look at the strategies more closely, we should first look at an important aspect of pivot calculation.

Image 2: USDCAD weekly pivots from 09.30to 10.18.2019

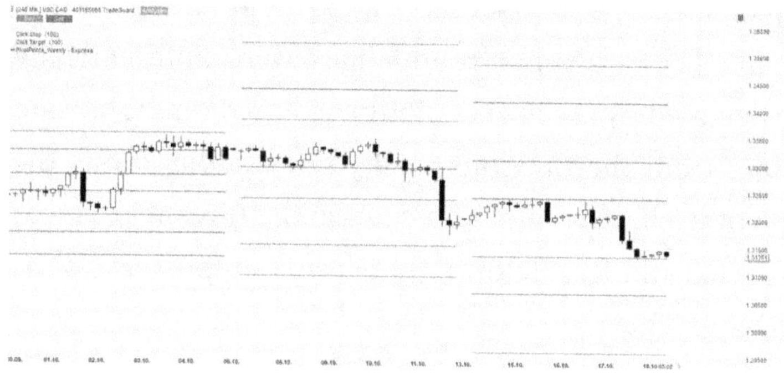

Take a closer look at Image 2. It shows the pivot lines for the three weeks from September 30 to October 18, for the USDCAD currency pair. It is easy to see that the pivot lines are close together in the week from 09.30 to 10.04 (on the left of the chart). The distance between the individual lines that week was barely 30 pips. It speaks for itself that scalping strategies aimed at targets of 15 or even 20 pips are difficult to implement here. We will see why this is so when we take a closer look at the two strategies.

In the week from 10.06 to 10.11 the levels were much wider. This was due to the fact that the volatility had suddenly increased in the previous week. And, because the new pivot lines are calculated on the basis of the closing data from the previous week, the pivot lines for the second week were much wider. Here, the distance between the pivot and the R1 was 87 pips. This is, of course, much better for trading. In the following week (week from 10.13 to 10.18) it was already over 100 pips.

So, the trader will have to adjust his price targets to these conditions if he wants to be successful with his scalping strategies. For example, it makes no sense to work with price targets of 20 pips if the distance between the pivot and R1 is only 40 pips. The two strategies will clarify the reason for this. If the distance is 87 pips, as in the second week in figure 2, price targets of 20 pips seem to make sense to me.

Another reason why the trader should avoid weeks with narrow pivot lines is the fact that pivots are often hardly noticed by market participants in such weeks. If you look at the first week in figure 2 again, you can see that USDCAD started a rally slightly above S1 on October 2, which took the pair almost to R3 within a few hours. On the way, the pair splashed the pivot, R1 and R2, and then almost reached R3. This is good when the trader is working with strategies that rely on reaching the pivot lines fast. Of course, it is not that good if he is aiming for the opposite.

In the first case, it seems to be favorable at first, because the market reaches the price target quickly. However, if you only have a range of 30 pips, the problem is to find a reasonable entry point. Where do you want to enter if the distance between the pivot and R1 is only 35 pips, especially if you are working with price targets of 15 or even 20 pips?

As a general rule, I would avoid ranges smaller than 60 pips. With 60 pips you can at least work with price targets of 15 pips, because they correspond to ¼ of the range. That makes sense in my eyes. I wouldn't touch anything underneath that.

Most pivot traders in Forex work with daily pivots. That is, with pivot levels that are calculated every day, on the basis of the price data of the "previous day", although strictly speaking there is no such thing in Forex. Reason enough for me not to do this. I prefer to trade the weekly pivots, mainly because I feel they are more reliable than the daily pivots. By this, I mean that the levels that were built based on the previous week's data are more likely to be considered by the big players than the levels of the previous day.

Thus, the two strategies try <u>to trade short-term trades based on medium-term data.</u> This may sound rather unorthodox to some traders, but we will see from the examples that such an approach can be quite profitable.

Strategy 1: Trade the Pivot

This strategy is a variation of the first strategy with the round number, but here, we apply it to the weekly pivots. As the example in Figure 1 clearly shows, market participants tend to respect weekly pivot levels *at the first touch*. And the remark "at the first touch" is therefore significant. The trader should only trade the first touch. He can safely refrain from further touches with the same pivot line.

In three of the four cases in Figure 1, the market reached the pivot level almost exactly, whereupon the market turned in the other direction. We want to take advantage of this fact in this strategy, by placing limit orders at the pivot levels and speculating on a countermove of 15 pips. Again, we use bracket orders, where, once the trade has been executed, an automatic stop order and an automatic take profit order become active in the market. So nothing is left to chance. Again, the parameters are clear and easy to understand. We set a price target of 15 pips with a risk of 15 pips as well. This means that we are working with a risk-reward ratio of 1:1. That said, the strategy must achieve a hit rate higher than 50% in order to be profitable. First of all, let's look at an example of the strategy.

<h1 align="center">Figure 3: USDCAD,
15-minute chart, October 7, 2019</h1>

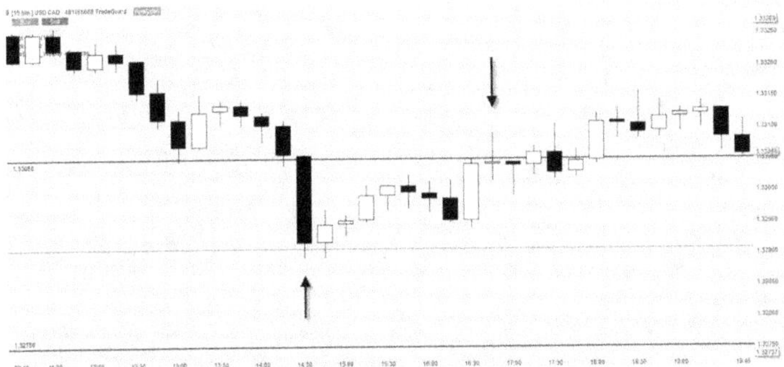

In this example, the trader expected the USDCAD pair to turn at the pivot and make at least a 15 pip countermove. The middle line on the image represents the pivot for this week. It was at 1.3290. The buy limit was waiting here. The upper line represents the price target, which was 15 pips higher, at 1.3305. The lower horizontal line was the stop level, at 1.3275. As the example shows, USDCAD reached the pivot at 14.30 (European time) and turned almost exactly (downward arrow, left). The pair reached the price target at 16:45 (upward arrow, right). The trade was never in danger.

We will now look at two weeks of "trading the pivot" in the USDJPY currency pair.

Figure 4: USDJPY, hourly chart 09.22 to 10.04.2019

The trader had two excellent weeks in USDJPY. In total, he was able to execute eight trades – four in each week. In the chart, I marked the profitable trades with the letter W (Win), and the loss trades with L (Loss). There was only one loss, on October 2. Here, the market hit the stop. I marked the last trade of the first week as B, or break even. This trade barely moved, and could therefore be classified as a break even trade, because the trader closed it at the entry price. The result of two weeks of trading in USDJPY looks like this:

Profitable trades: 6 x 15 pips   = 90 pips
Loss trades: 1 x 15 pips   = -15 pips
Breakeven Trades: 1 x 0 pips   =   0 pips
Total: **75 pips**

Of course, those are excellent results, but as the next example in Figure 5 shows, it does not always run that smoothly.

Figure 5: USDJPY, hourly chart 07.15 to 07.16.2019

In these two weeks, the market only touched the pivot or the resistance/support lines four times. And only one of these touches led to success. The other three resulted in losses. Obviously, the market participants were less inclined to respect the weekly pivots during this period, even at the first touch, which often leads to a bounce in the other direction, which, in turn, is the premise of this strategy.

The question of whether one should trade again could arise, if the trade was stopped at the first attempt and the market takes a fresh start on the targeted pivot line. I would be cautious here. If the market hits the stop on the first attempt, this is usually a sign that "the market" is not particularly concerned about the weekly pivots. In my experience, it is better to wait until a new opportunity arises on another pivot line, either up or down.

With these kinds of strategies, you have to realize that patience pays off. As you can see in Figure 5, sometimes a currency pair does not do so well for two weeks. But that does not mean that the strategy does not work in the long run. Figure 4 shows that you can sometimes achieve pretty good results. If you take the results of Image 4 and Image 5 together, you get a realistic assessment of the strategy.

Profitable trades: 7 x 15 pips	=	105 pips
Loss trades: 4 x 15 pips	=	-60 pips
Breakeven Trades: 1 x 0 pips	=	0 pips
Total:		**45 pips**

So, the total result of four weeks of trading in USDJPY would be 45 pips. This would give the strategy a total hit rate of 58.33%. The trader achieved an average result of 3.75 pips per trade. This may not be a very spectacular result, but it is realistic in my eyes.

If a trader wants to achieve a total monthly target of 100 pips, under these conditions he must execute at least 26 trades (3.75 x 26.66 = 100 pips). If we take the number of 12 trades in USDJPY as an average, he would have to execute the strategy in at least seven other currency pairs to get the desired result.

However, we should act with caution here. Experienced forex traders know that if one currency pair does not perform particularly well, often, the other currency pairs do not either. Therefore, I would not advise you to use the same strategy on such a large number of "different" currency pairs. All currency pairs are strongly correlated. This means that they often show similar results. One should also remember that the dollar is always involved, either directly or indirectly. Even if the currency pair does not bear the term "dollar" in its name, as is the case with **GBPJPY** or **EURCHF**, the strength or weakness of the dollar always has an influence.

In other words, the more currency pairs you trade with a similar strategy, the bigger the so-called *cluster risk* becomes. This risk occurs when you are unilaterally invested in too many instruments of the same asset class.

I would rather advise you to spread the risk by no longer adding currency pairs to one strategy, but rather by trading different strategies with different price

Strategy 2:
The "last 20 Pips" Strategy

Just like the stop-hunting strategy with the round number, the last 20 pips strategy is based on the assumption that, when the market approaches one of the weekly pivots, it will usually reach it. This means that momentum traders will drive the pair towards the weekly pivot once it is only a few pips away from it. In this sense, the last 20 pips strategy is a momentum strategy, because it relies on the final momentum that arises as soon as the price appears to be near the pivot level.

The reason this happens is basically the same as with the round number strategy. The pivot lines, and especially the weekly pivot lines, exert a "magnetic force" on the prices as they approach them. In addition, market participants assume that the market will turn as soon as it reaches this level.

This happens all the more when the market is in a sideways phase. Many traders consider pivot levels to be price targets for existing trades. Of course, they can also use them as entry levels. In that case they would execute countertrend trades, such as the "trade the pivot" strategy, which I covered in the first part.

When the trader decides to use the "last 20 pips", strategy he tries to profit from the last 20 pips before the market reaches the pivot level. Here our price target is waiting in the form of a take profit order. Usually, I use a profit target of 20 pips. Of course, I can vary this if the currency pair requires it (for example, in less volatile times or when the pair itself is not fluctuating much). In that case, I would rather work with a price target of 15 pips.

However, I avoid currency pairs with a low daily fluctuation, such as the AUDUSD or NZDUSD in September 2019. Here, you would have to lower the price target to such an extent that the strategy could hardly be profitable anymore. It is not impossible to trade these pairs if you have excellent broker conditions. But, we have enough other tradable currency pairs, so why make it difficult?

With this strategy, I once again work with a risk reward ratio (RRR) of 1:1. The reason is simple. I assume that if the market is approaching the pivot level by 20 pips, it is more likely to be attracted to the pivot level, rather than taking another detour in the other direction.

Thus, we know that we need a hit rate higher than 50%, in order to trade profitably. I am well aware that such a goal is not always easy to achieve. However, my experience is that it can be achieved if the trader implements the strategy in a disciplined manner. For this to succeed, a strategy must be logical and as simple as possible.

Figure 6: USD/JPY, 15 minute chart, 09.12.2019

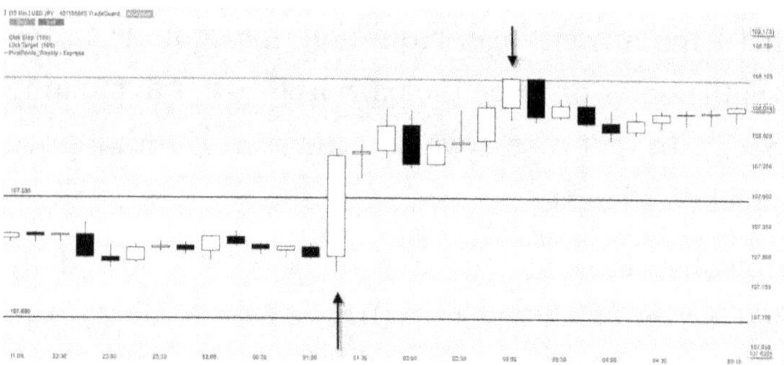

The example on the 15-minute chart of the USD/JPY (Fig. 6) illustrates the strategy. The upper horizontal line represents the R2 level (Resist 2). It was at 108.09 in that week, and this was the target price for the trade. The middle line was 20 pips below R2, and this represented the entry level at 107.89. This entry was activated when the USD/JPY reached this level (arrow, bottom left). Finally, the stop-loss level was waiting 20 pips lower, at 107.69 (horizontal line, downward). As you can see on the chart, the market reached the price target pretty quickly (upward arrow, right), while the market did not touch the stop level.

This is not always the case, as is shown in the example below, in the USDCAD hourly chart.

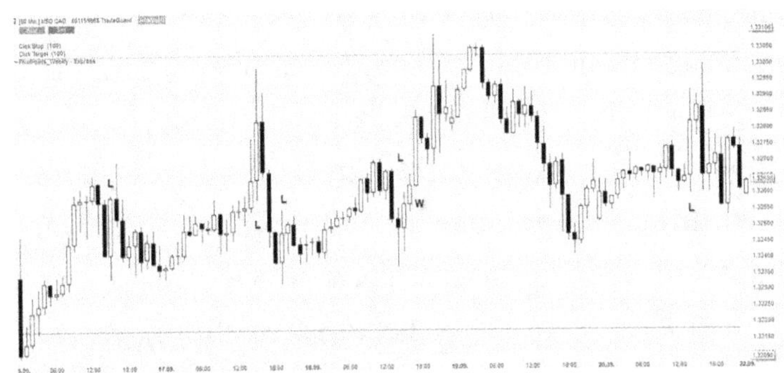

In the week from September 15 to September 22, 2019, the USDCAD oscillated between the pivot level (horizontal line, below) and the R1 (horizontal line, above). This happens quite often. Forex markets will rarely reach the weekly R3 or S3 pivot. This usually happens when the pair shows more of a trend behavior. Since we know that forex markets tend to trade sideways most of the time, trading will mostly take place around the weekly pivot. Price targets are then usually R1 or S1, or the pivot itself, as in Figure 7.

After all, the trader was able to make 6 trades in this week, but only one of them was profitable, and five of them led to a loss. These were the results:

Profitable Trades: 1 x 20 pips =   20 pips

Loss trades: 5 x 20 pips   = -100 pips

Total: **-80 pips**

The trader suffered a loss of -80 pips in this currency pair. This is, of course, an unsatisfactory result, but it is perfectly normal. Every trader has such weeks, and at the same time, it should be a warning to those traders who believe that you can make money easily in forex. Nothing is farther from the truth. Forex trading is like any other form of trading – it is hard work. Only those who execute their strategy(ies) in a disciplined manner have a chance of being successful. If you are confronted with such "unlucky weeks", you can also experience weeks where things go like clockwork, as the example below in Figure 8 illustrates.

Figure 8: USD/CAD, hourly chart, August 18 to September 1, 2019

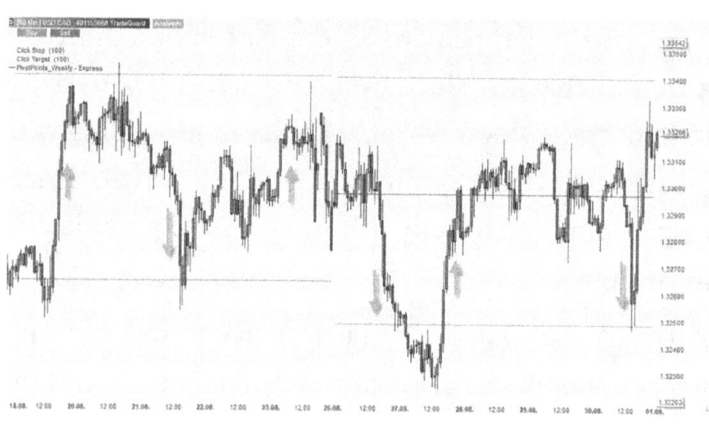

In the two weeks from August 18, 2019 to September 1, 2019, the trader was able to execute six trades, all six of which ran into profit (arrows in the chart). Of course, one wishes it would always be that way.

With regard to the 20 pips profit target, the trader should remain flexible. If the distance between the pivot and the R1 is 60 pips or less, it makes no sense to work with a price target of 20 pips. Here, 15 pips should do it. If the distance between the two levels becomes even smaller, you should stop trading the strategy.

If we add the results of Image 7 and Image 8 together, we get a realistic idea of what forex trading is really all about.

Profitable trades: 7 x 20 pips = 140 pips
Loss trades: 5 x 20 pips   = -100 pips
Total: **40 pips**

Is a profit of 40 a good result for three weeks of trading? Answer: Yes Sir. It is good.

Should I change the parameters if trading isn't going well?

As a final remark, I would like to briefly answer the question of whether it makes sense to change the parameters of the two strategies, in order to get a better result. As an example, the trader might get the idea of working with a price target of 20 pips and a stop loss of only 15. In this way, he would increase the overall results of his winners. Of course, that is true. At the same time, however, with this measure, he would probably reduce his hit rate. Instead of a hit rate of 58%, he would then suddenly be able to achieve only 54%, or even less. Thus, the final result would not change much.

Of course, you can consider changing the parameters of a system, and let's be honest, every trader does exactly that if things don't go so well for a while. The question is whether turning the parameter screw is the best solution in such a situation. Unfortunately, this measure distorts your statistics, the continuous analysis of which is so important for building a profitable trading business (and also for convincing potential investors).

In my opinion, it is better to ignore drawdowns that drag on for a few weeks, and continue trading the system "stoically". Should it turn out, after an extended period, that profitability is not returning, one should seriously consider taking the strategy off the market.

Changing the parameters prematurely in case of temporary losses usually indicates an amateur trader. Often it is the trader who trades one single strategy, who does this. If you only have one active strategy, you are much more dependent on the results of that strategy.

Professionals (hedge funds and other institutional investors) typically go for <u>a variety of strategies</u>, and compare them with each other. If one of them performs a little less effectively (and there may always be one or more that are not performing as well), then they compare the results with historical data or with the results of the strategies that are performing well. Professionals don't get nervous because they have had some losses in a particular currency pair for two or three weeks.

PART 3:
TRADING WITH THE
WEEKLY HIGH AND LOW

Introduction to trading with the weekly high and low

Just like the pivot points and the round number, the highs and lows of the past days or weeks represent significant levels in the chart, that are noticed by many market participants. For day traders, of course, the highs and lows of the previous day are of particular importance. If the market goes above or below these levels, it gives the trader a signal that it is leaving the previous day's range.

These price points are even more important if we look at the *weekly timeframe*. After all, the high of the previous week means that this was the highest price that traders were willing to pay for a particular currency pair. The same is true, of course, for the previous week's low. This was the lowest price that traders were still willing to pay for the pair. On no other day of the previous week did anybody pay a higher or lower price.

If the market approaches a similar price level again in the following week, it automatically attracts the attention of market participants, because, when this happens, the question arises as to whether or not the market will turn again at the same level (as in the previous week), or whether, this time, the market will break through this price level and whether this event will possibly end last week's range?

Such an event is quite significant. It can mean the beginning of a new trend or the continuation of an existing one. No wonder, then, that these price levels attract the attention of market participants. And whatever attracts attention automatically generates the interest of those traders who like to jump on trains that are racing in a certain direction at full speed. These are the so-called momentum traders, who want to profit from the attraction of such levels.

Therefore, it makes sense – in analogy to the strategies with the round number and the pivots – to develop tactics that take advantage of this situation.

If the market only falls below the previous week's high briefly, the question arises as to whether or not it is more likely to be attracted by it. And secondly, the question is whether the market will continue to move when it reaches this level, or whether it will first push it back a few pips. The two strategies presented here deal with exactly this issue.

Here, as everywhere else in Forex trading, the following question arises: is there a higher probability that this scenario or another one will occur in the long run?

If the probability is only slightly higher than the opposite probability, we know that we have gained a small advantage over "the market".

If this is not possible, and the efficiency theory of the market supporters turns out to be right, even considering dealing with Forex trading would, of course, be pointless from the outset.

Forex trading is nothing more than gaining a small advantage, which we call an *edge*. For Forex traders, it is therefore important that one scenario or another, which has a higher probability than its opposite number, will arise. For outsiders, this may seem insignificant. But a trader knows that this small difference can be the basis of a profitable trading business.

Strategy 1:
Chase the Weekly High and Low

The first strategy deals with the attraction that a previous week's high or low has on the price. We start with the observation that, as soon as the current price is only a few pips away from these levels, it will automatically be attracted by them, like metal to a powerful magnet. The "Chase the weekly high and low strategy" assumes that there is a higher probability that the market will move towards this level rather than in the opposite direction. Figure 1 illustrates the principle of the strategy.

Figure 1: USDJPY, 15-minute chart, 10/15/2019

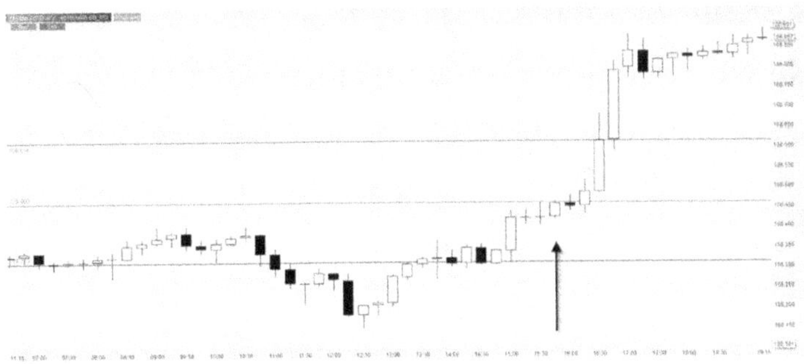

In this example, with USDJPY, the previous week's high was 108.61 (upper horizontal line). After initially moving sideways on October 15, the market approached this level shortly after the start of American trading, at around 15:30 European time. As a result, the stop buy order was executed at 108.46 (middle horizontal line and arrow on the chart). Somewhat later, the price reached the previous week's high. The position was closed, thanks to an automatic take profit order, with a profit of 15 pips.

The lower horizontal line, at 108.31, represents the level where the stop loss order was waiting. As you can clearly see, the trade was never in danger. Since the trader was working with a bracket order, the stop-loss order was automatically closed when the market reached the target price.

As with the first four strategies in this series, we work with a risk reward ratio of 1:1, risking 15 pips to gain 15 pips, because we believe that in the majority of cases, the price will reach the price target sooner than the stop-loss order.

Now, of course, "probability" also means that in many cases, this will not happen. The trader will therefore have to take loss trades into account in this strategy – as is the case for every strategy.

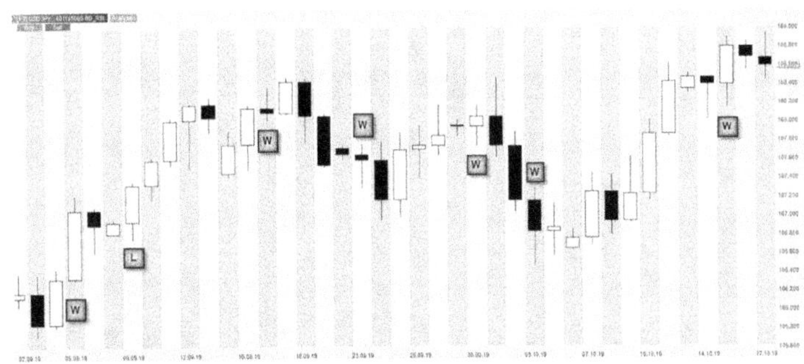

The daily chart of the USDJPY currency pair illustrates the number of trades that you will realistically get with this strategy. In total, the pair reached seven times the previous week's low or high. In six of the seven cases the trade reached the price target. Only once, on September 9 was there a loss. For this period, the result is as follows:

Profit trades: 6 x 15 pips   = 90 pips
Loss trades: 1 x 15 pips   = -15 pips

Total: **75 pips**

This is, of course, an excellent result, but it should not always be assumed in this strategy.

<h1 align="center">Figure 3: USDCAD,
daily chart, 20.09 to 20.10.2019</h1>

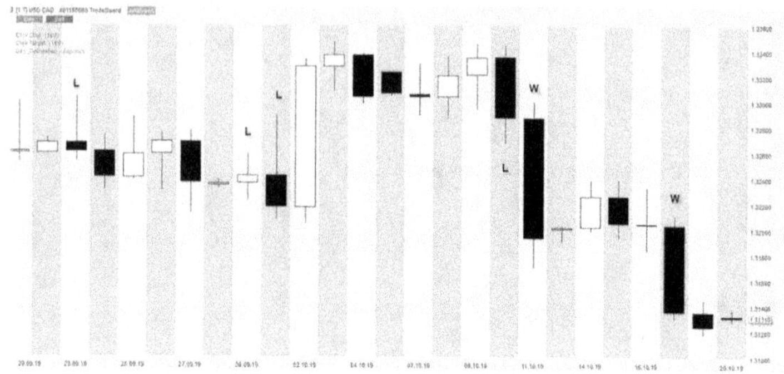

Figure 3, in contrast, clearly illustrates what trading can mean. During this period, the trader executed six trades in USDCAD, four of which were losers. The result was as follows:

Profit trades: 2 x 15 pips	= 30 pips
Loss trades: 4 x 15 pips	= -60 pips
Total:	**-30 pips**

If we add up the results of the two trading periods (Figures 2 and 3), we get the following final result:

Profit trades: 8 x 15 pips	= 120 pips
Loss trades: 5 x 15 pips	= -75 pips
Total:	**45 pips**

Now, a beginner might be disappointed by such a "result" after a month and a half of forex trading. But as I said before, I attribute this to the exaggerated expectations that haunt many Forex forums. Forex trading is a business, just like any other, and it must therefore be treated and seen as such. It is a well-known fact that "losses" in trading should be seen as nothing more than "costs". The trader has to bear these costs so that he can participate in the market. He has to "pay" with his losses, so to speak, in order to be able to participate at all.

If there is one thing I want to achieve with this book, it is to ensure that the reader gets <u>a realistic assessment of what Forex trading means,</u> but I also want to show traders what they can achieve. In my opinion, these 45 pips are quite sufficient to build a successful trading business.

Now, the reader might object, stating that this strategy does not give enough signals. This is true – it is a consequence of the fact that the strategy works with the previous week's highs and lows. By no means does the market reach those levels every time. Moreover, there are also weeks in which it neither touches the high nor the low of the previous week (so-called inside-weeks). Precisely for this reason, the trader should not only apply the strategy to one currency pair, but to several, and he should combine it with the other strategies.

Strategy 2:
Weekly High and Low Stretch

Finally, we will take a look at the second strategy, which works with the previous weeks' highs and lows. My research and tests have shown that Forex markets like to stage "a slight exaggeration" when reaching these levels. What do I mean by this? In contrast to round number strategies and pivots, I have observed that the market tends to overshoot at such levels. The reason is simple: many institutional traders have placed buy orders (or sell orders for lows) in these places. When the market reaches such a level, these orders become active. This causes a certain buying pressure when the market reaches the previous week's high. However, the opposite can also happen. If the market arrives at the previous week's low, the additional sell orders create selling pressure. A scalper can profit from this effect. And this is what the second strategy is all about.

With the Weekly High and Low Stretch strategy, the trader only enters the market when it touches the previous week's level (high or low). He assumes that there is a higher probability that the market will exaggerate a bit, at least in the short term, before a possible turn. We want to use this effect to bet on 15 pips. We therefore bet on a short-term exaggeration of 15 pips at the first touch. Again, we protect our position with a stop-loss of 15 pips. So again, we are working with a risk reward ratio of 1:1, which means that our hit rate must be above 50%, in order to trade profitably.

The premise of this strategy –in contrast to the round number and pivot strategies – is therefore the observation that once the market has reached the previous week's highs or lows, it will run a little further before turning. If the trade does not succeed the first time, and the market makes a second attempt to exceed this level, the probability that the second trade will go up is not as high. Therefore I emphasize <u>the importance of the first touch</u>.

Figure 4: USDCAD, 15-minute chart, October 17, 2019

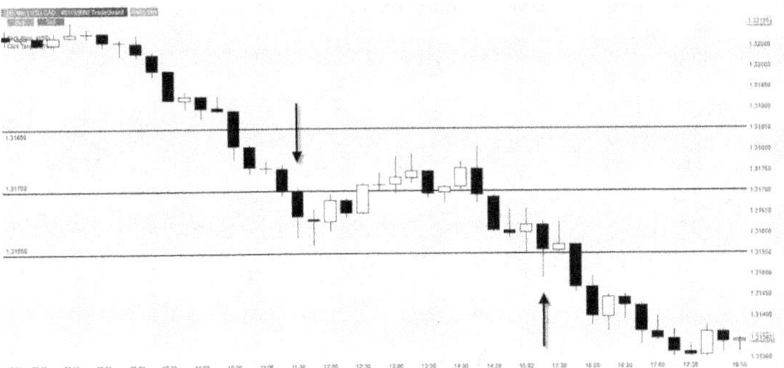

Figure 4 illustrates the strategy in the 15-minute chart of USDCAD. The middle horizontal line represents the previous week's low at 1.3170. On October 17, USDCAD traded above the previous week's low. However, the pair then fell throughout the European morning, reaching the previous week's low at 11:15 am. At that moment, the waiting short sell order became active (upper left arrow). At the same time, the Stop Loss Order (upper horizontal line) and the Take Profit Order (lower horizontal line) were activated. At 15:15, the price reached the target of 15 pips (bottom right arrow).

As you can see, USDJPY took some time and also rose a bit after reaching the previous week's low. However, the market did not hit the stop-loss order. As a result, the trade never got into trouble, and it reached the price target at 1.3155.

As already mentioned, the nature of this strategy is that the trader will only receive signals from time to time. The market does not reach the previous high or low every week. If it reaches neither the low nor the high, we speak of "inside weeks." In this case, nothing happens with our strategy, and on Friday, the trader has to take the bracket orders he placed at the previous week's high and low out of the market.

Of course, I tried the "opposite" of this strategy, namely taking the opposite position as soon as the market reaches the previous week's high or low. In that case you would go short at the previous week's high and long at the previous week's low. The results were disappointing for all currency pairs. I did not achieve a single positive result in any of the currencies, over a period of several months. On the other hand, the "Weekly High Low Stretch Strategy" was very successful, and produced more gains than losses. This does not mean, however, that this will always be the case. Situations may well arise, in which the first scenario is more successful than the "stretch strategy" presented here.

I cannot stress enough, that a trader should always look at the markets with an open mind. Even if he has successfully executed certain strategies over a long period of time, the day may well come, when this is suddenly no longer the case. At that moment, it can be quite useful to try the opposite of what you have been doing all along. The results I am presenting here in **USDJPY** and **USDCAD** should therefore be considered as a snapshot. This is by no means a guarantee that they will turn out equally well in the future.

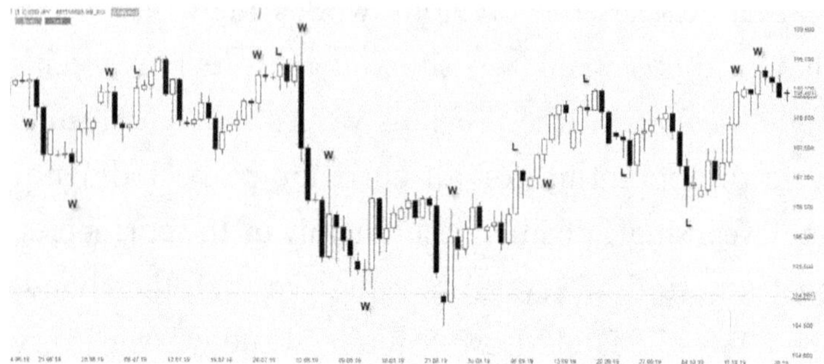

Over a period of about four months, the trader received seventeen signals in the USDJPY currency pair. Eleven of them were profit trades and only six were loss trades. Of course, this is an excellent result, which should not always be taken for granted. As you can see, with this strategy, you get an average of one signal per week. That is not much, and that is why it should be combined with other strategies, such as the Chase the Weekly High Low strategy.

Finally, let us look at the results of the strategy in the USDCAD currency pair. I deliberately chose the same period as I used in the example for the USDJPY. The results in USDCAD were also excellent. Here I received sixteen signals, of which eleven were profit trades (W) and only five were loss trades (L).

If you add the results in both currency pairs together, you get the following results:

Profit trades: 22 x 15 pips = 330 pips
Loss trades: 11 x 15 pips   = -165 pips

Total: **165 pips**

Of course, an overall result of 165 pips is very good. Even if this profit was made over a period of four months.

One could now get the idea that a cluster risk could arise if one were to trade the same strategy on a number of highly correlated currency pairs. I am well aware of this. However, I have not been able to identify this kind of risk. The weekly highs and lows in different currency pairs were reached on different days, so the signals did not occur on the same day in all of the traded pairs. Of course, one should not trade too many pairs with this one strategy. In that case, a cluster risk would indeed occur, if the trader were to trade too many similar or highly correlated pairs.

Practical questions

Finally, I would like to address some questions that arise when the trader applies both strategies in reality.

In general, you should not place a trade if the market on Sunday evening (or Monday morning) is trading at the same level as the previous week's high or low. It makes no sense to trade the stretch strategy or the chase the weekly high and low strategy if the market is only ten or even twenty pips below or above these levels. It is better to wait until the market is at least forty or fifty pips away, and then place your orders for the week.

It does not matter if you trade the "high" from "below" or from "above". What do I mean by this? It is quite common for a pair to open above the previous week's high at the beginning of the week. For example, this can happen during strong trends. You do not have to give up on the strategy just because the market has already opened above the high. You can certainly trade this high from the short side. The same applies if the market opens below the previous weekly low. Here, you can definitely try a long trade with a price target of a weekly low. Or you can use the stretch strategy to bet on the exaggeration.

However, these cases are rather rare, and every now and then, there are inside weeks, in which the market reaches neither the high nor the low.

If you trade both strategies on the same number of currency pairs at the same time, it is advisable to use two different broker accounts. Just to avoid confusion. This method also makes you less dependent on a single broker. Professional traders usually have several accounts with different brokers. I think this is a measure that should be implemented for risk management reasons alone. Spread your trading capital over two or three broker accounts, rather than having everything in one account.

Imagine you have all your money parked in one broker account, and suddenly the broker gets into financial trouble. You may think that this is very unlikely, but experience has shown that, especially in extreme events such as the Swiss franc shock of 2015, poorly capitalized brokers can easily go bankrupt. Protect your trading capital from such an event. As a rule, the trader will get his money back some time, if he has a segregated account (which I strongly recommend). A segregated account is an account that is held separately from the broker's assets, in the name (and ownership) of the trader. Nevertheless, this "some time" may well extend to two years or more. So, make sure that you never get into such a situation and find yourself unable to trade for two years, because your money is "blocked" due to exceptional circumstances. Bankruptcy proceedings can sometimes drag on for years.

Spreading your trading capital across multiple accounts makes your trading business less vulnerable to external risks.

However, the most important measure, that will certainly make your trading business robust, is <u>if you stop trading just one strategy</u>. By presenting six different strategies in this series on Forex trading, I am not suggesting that you should trade them separately, but rather, that you should *combine* them. The reason why you should do this will be dealt with in the fourth and final part of this series.

PART 4:
TRADE SEVERAL STRATEGIES SIMULTANEOUSLY

1. Why you should trade several strategies at once!

Traders who specialize in forex trading tend to trade *only one strategy* at a time. I know this too well! I was once such a trader myself (at that time, currency trading was a new, hot thing for private investors). And that was when I made the first mistake, which, in my ignorance, I unfortunately repeated again and again. Because if you only have one strategy, you are inevitably <u>constantly looking for the one strategy that will make you rich.</u>

Have a look at the trader forums on the internet. They are full of threads by traders who present their strategy – of course, with the best intentions. With every new strategy that appears there, the forex community gets into a frenzy and everyone jumps on this new bandwagon. Everybody has to try this new thing out right away, because this could be where the gold that everyone is looking for is buried.

What comes next, I hardly need to tell the reader. No sooner has the forum member tried out the new strategy when the first losing trades start to appear after a few winning trades. Maybe the new thing is not as promising as it looked at first glance. Soon, the forum member comes to realize that, unfortunately, the new strategy generates as many losses as the previous one.

And so the train goes on, and the next day the forum member will try out the strategy of Forum Member X, which he has overlooked thus far. I think the reader now already knows how the story ends. The unhappy forum member will now "test" the strategy of Forum Member X and after a few weeks he will realize that the gold is not buried there either.

This brings us to a conclusion that is hardly surprising: <u>all forex strategies make losses</u>. All of them! Some a bit more, some a bit less. And this brings us to a second conclusion: <u>all (or almost all) forex strategies are profitable</u>.

I beg your pardon. All Forex strategies are profitable? Yes, most, or at least many of these strategies (if they are based on well-proven trading principles) are profitable in the long run, at least, if they obey simple mathematical laws – in trader's language: if they work with risk reward ratios of 1:2 or 1:3. And even if they work with risk reward ratios of only 1:1, but with hit rates of over 50%, all these systems are profitable in the long run.

Mind you: in the long run. And here, of course, lies the problem of our eager forum member. If he starts testing the system in a period where it is currently in a drawdown phase, he will discard it after a few weeks (or a few days). He will write in the forum thread that the system of Forum Member X only produces losses. Let's look at the capital curve of this forex strategy (Figure 1).

Figure 1: Capital curve of forum member X

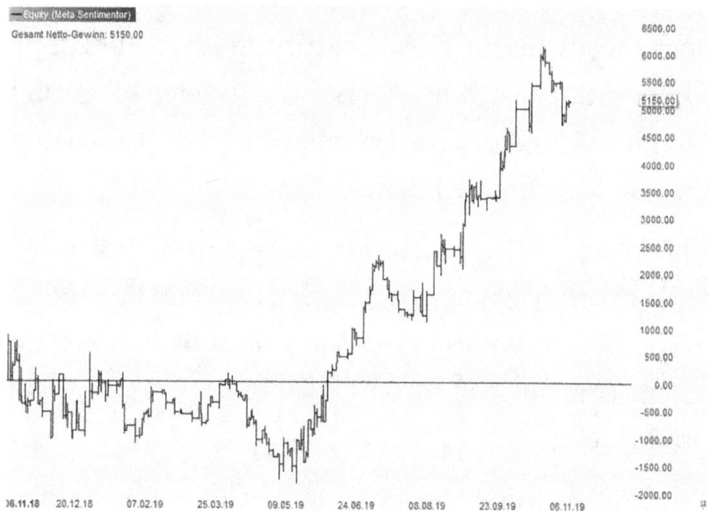

Is this strategy profitable? It certainly is! With the results of this simple strategy, you can make a fortune (if you want to). But did you also look at the drawdown period from November 2018 to May 2019 (left in the chart)? This lasted seven months! Think about it: seven months in which the system did not generate any profits!

Now ask yourself: As a human being, can you stand it if the system you are trading does not generate any profits or even losses for more than seven months? Probably not, right? I cannot stand it under any circumstances.

Why not? Because I am human. Unfortunately, our psyche is such that we are always looking for instant gratification. That means that when we ask for something, we want it *immediately*.

I am a coffee drinker. Now imagine I go to my favorite coffee house and ask for a cup of coffee. The waitress tells me in a somewhat hushed voice that unfortunately there is no coffee today (because the espresso machine needs servicing, or for whatever reason). I make a face and, for better or worse, I choose to drink tea. The next day I go there again. I am looking forward for my favorite coffee, but when the waitress approaches me, I already suspect it. Unfortunately the espresso machine is still being serviced.

Will I go back to that coffee house the next day? Probably not, right? Maybe the espresso machine at the neighbors' shop works better. Unfortunately, this means that we, as human beings, are so predisposed that we cannot stand too many rejections – although we know very well that the espresso machine in our favorite coffee house will work again sooner or later. It has to, otherwise the shop will soon lose all its customers. We know that, and yet we prefer to go to the coffee house next door, because as coffee addicts, we simply cannot stand having to drink tea three days in a row.

This little story may seem a bit simple to you, but that is what happens to your reptilian brain when you enter the forex market and make a trade. The dear forum member hurries from coffee house to coffee house (from strategy to strategy, so to speak) in the hope of finally finding the coffee house where he is guaranteed a coffee every day.

You already know the end of the song. The dear forum member will ride this carousel until his "trading capital" is exhausted. This day will come sooner or later (usually sooner), and then, of course, you can predict what comes next: a disgruntled claim that "forex does not work".

Right. Forex trading is virtually unpredictable in the short term. It is impossible to say that if you are trading System X or System Y from today, you will be successful right away. Within the space of a few weeks (let alone days), this is almost impossible to say. And unfortunately our reptilian brain is only able to evaluate something based on such short time spans. We are simply not able to use our human brain to evaluate a trading system that produces quite robust results in the long run (see Figure 1).

And this fact alone is the most important reason <u>why you should not rely on a single strategy</u> if you plan to build a trading business based on currency trading. It makes you incredibly vulnerable. Unfortunately, too often it happens that a trader drops a profitable strategy just because it produces losses for a few weeks.

If you trade with only one strategy, you will be exposed to so many pitfalls and traps that you will constantly trip yourself up.

There are, of course, several reasons why traders trade with only one strategy. The main reason is probably that they believe it is superior to other trading methods. When traders start out in forex trading, they usually use the method they first came across (i.e. by chance). They use this method because they still understand very little about trading. And of course, because they are not really aware that there are other profitable methods or systems.

When this system produces its first losses, they gradually lose confidence, thinking that their system will never give them the desired result. And inevitably, they will look around the forex forum again, and try out the system suggested by Forum Member Y or Z. Once they have "tested" Methods Y or Z, they immediately believe that they must be better than their own method. They come to this conclusion because they have just started trading this new method. They are still hopeful that it will give them the desired results.

Many forex traders, for example, have switched to trading "price action strategies" in recent years. You could see this trend emerging a few years ago. One trader started it, some followed suit, and all of a sudden, all of the trader forums were full of "price action".

Do not get me wrong. I am not criticizing this method. It is a robust trading method, based on some simple and clear principles. There is a clear trading philosophy behind it. But there is no reason to assume that price action is better than any other method, for example, one that is simply based on crossing two indicators or on continuation patterns in trend phases. All these methods are based on a specific observation of market behavior. And none of them are wrong. But neither are they any "better".

The reason why a trader switches from one method to another is often simple, for example because one method seems to be more "obvious" to him than the other. In my opinion, this is the reason for the success of the price action method. It makes sense to many traders, because it is easy to understand. But that does not mean that it is more profitable than any other method.

Each strategy therefore has its own premises about how the market works. For a price action trader, all the information can be found in the chart itself. This means that he does not use any technical analysis instruments, such as indicators or oscillators. And for a trader who trades support and resistance, it is precisely the observation that there are simply more sellers at resistance levels than elsewhere.

Another important reason why traders only commit to a single strategy is <u>because a single strategy makes it easier to understand the market</u>. It is in the nature of our brains that we try to simplify things when we are faced with complexity. We want to understand what is going on in the financial markets. But we try to do this by using simplified models and deliberately overlooking other models.

Now, the financial markets are the most complex systems imaginable. And the natural need to comprehend them by means of simplified models is only too understandable. But, the consequence is that you get a distorted picture of reality. Your method, the system you are trading, makes you believe that the market will do this or that, and you try to explain its behavior with your system. This inevitably leads to an incomplete picture of reality.

Most traders I know consider their strategies as independent systems, the returns of which are used to achieve their financial goals. If this is the case, <u>every strategy should basically be seen as a long-term bet on an expected outcome,</u> and in that sense, every strategy should basically be seen as a *security* in which you invest a certain amount of money. When you buy a stock, you hope for a certain return in the long run, either by speculating on the performance of that stock or by buying income from the investment that pays you an annual dividend.

In the same way, you should look at a certain strategy. You should look at it <u>as an investment security in your portfolio,</u> just like a stock or a fund.

If you can accept this idea, then investing in a certain strategy or in another asset is basically the same for you. The next step is to build an investment portfolio.

From now on, it is no longer a single investment (be it a single strategy or a single stock) that is the instrument for achieving your financial goals. From now on, you want to have a balanced portfolio with different assets.

Just as nobody would think of building an investment portfolio with only a single stock, you should not build a portfolio with *only one* strategy.

2. Less volatility in the capital curve

We can now rely on two areas that have been intensively researched in science and tested in practice for decades: portfolio optimization and diversification. By applying these fundamental principles, which are incorporated into the creation of a portfolio of common assets, we can create a portfolio of multiple strategy systems. The same benefits you get from a portfolio of common assets, such as lower volatility of the capital curve and a risk-adjusted return, can be applied to your portfolio of trading strategies.

You should also think the idea of a portfolio through to the end. Just as the manager of a large investment fund would not think of investing all of his clients' money in a single stock, he would not think of doing this when investing in trading strategies (which happens occasionally). He would never put all his eggs in one basket by trading just a single strategy. He will diversify.

In that sense, he cannot buy enough different assets. If he only bets on shares, he cannot own enough shares. Of course, such an approach carries certain risks. Ultimately, he wants to build a "balanced portfolio" – a portfolio in which opportunities and risks stand in a reasonable proportion to each other.

I am therefore convinced that <u>using several strategies is more profitable in the long run than trading just one strategy</u>. The reason is simple. If you trade several strategies at the same time, the probabilities of the individual strategies are distributed over time. Each strategy that you trade has its own set of profit and loss trades, as the examples in this book (Parts 1 to 3) have shown. As a trader, you just do not know when these series will occur, and in which of your strategies they are going to happen. The only thing you do know is that you will have these series of profit and loss.

By distributing profit and loss over several strategies, you create a certain indifference towards a loss series (better objectivity). This is of course easier to achieve with a portfolio consisting of several strategies, than if you were to trade a single strategy.

The selection of your strategies should ensure that the probabilities of profit or loss of the individual strategies are not mixed up. A trade made on the basis of pivots is quite different from a trade made on the basis of a round number or the previous week's high, for example. Although the probability exists, that all your strategies will take losses at the same time, this is rather unlikely.

If one of your strategies suddenly develops a losing streak, another could suddenly start to win. The differentiation effect then ensures that one winning series of a certain strategy compensates or cancels out the loss series of another strategy.

In other words, as a trader, you no longer concentrate on the execution of a single strategy (with all the psychological drawbacks). <u>From now on, you are the manager of a portfolio of different strategies</u>, which are hopefully correlated as little as possible. You will be applying the same principles as you would when managing a portfolio of traditional assets. The aim of this approach is to make your profit curve smoother and to limit your drawdowns. I would like to illustrate this with some examples.

Imagine that you are trading a portfolio of four forex strategies, all of which deliver different results.

**Figure 2: Strategy 1,
capital curve November 2018 - November 2019**

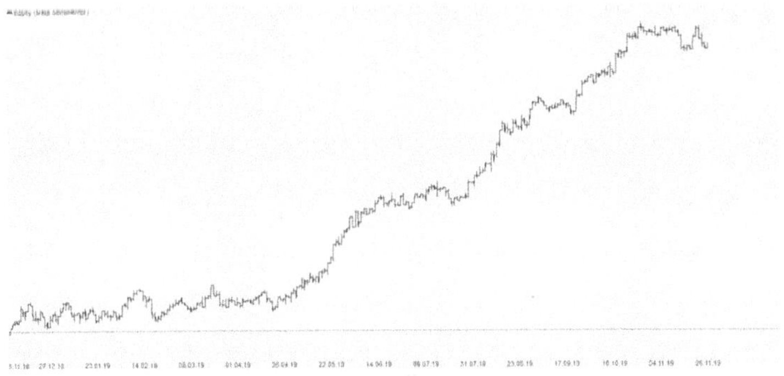

Your first strategy is quite profitable, as the capital curve of a whole year of trading (November 2018 - November 2019) shows. However, the profits did not come consistently. There was some profit in the first half of 2019, but it took until the end of April 2019 for the capital curve to start to pick up noticeably. A trader who traded this strategy exclusively would have probably retreated from it in disappointment after a few months, and stopped the strategy.

**Figure 3: Strategy 2,
capital curve November 2018 - November 2019**

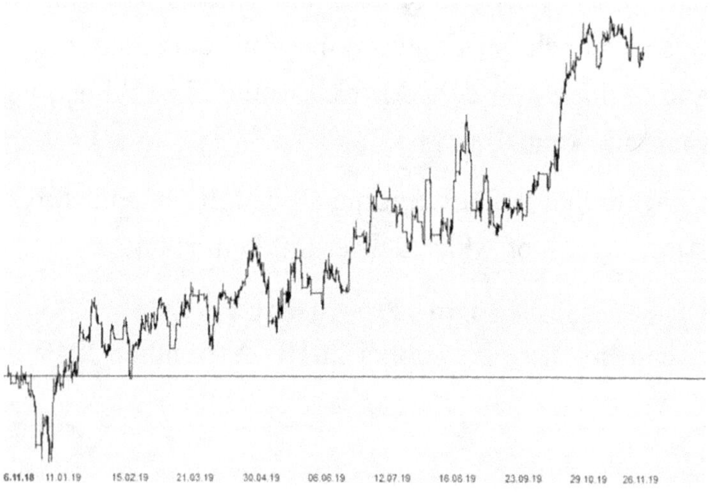

At first glance, the results of the second strategy seem to be easier for the trader psyche. However, the system started with a substantial drawdown (left side of the chart). It was in the red for over a month until it even started to produce profits. As you can see, it took almost until the summer of 2019 for the rising trend in the capital curve to become visible at all. Again, some would have given up after initially "disappointing results".

Figure 4: Strategy 3,
capital curve November 2018 - November 2019

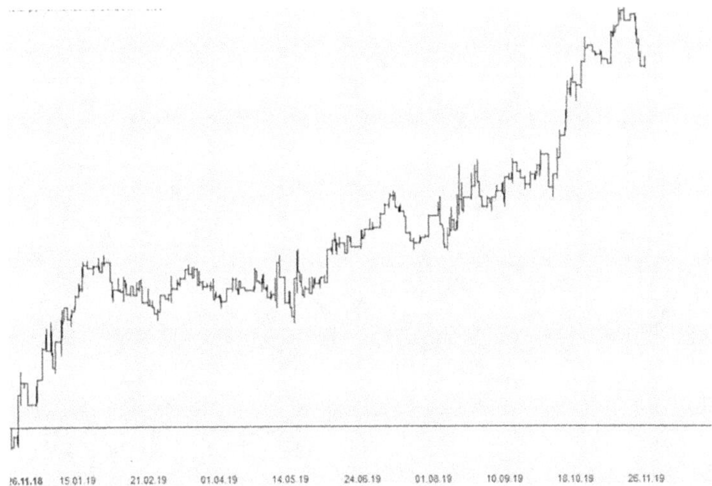

The third strategy certainly made it easier for the trader in the beginning, because the capital curve went straight up in the first weeks. But then, it wandered sideways for months (from February to May 2019) until, at some point, the capital curve reached a new "high." There was no drawdown in the true sense of the word, but from February to May, the system was not making any money. Again, patience only paid off gradually.

The fourth strategy produced significantly fewer trades than the first three, therefore the capital curve was quite volatile. The system produced repeated drawdowns of 40% and more over the course of the year. In September, the system even gave back a large part of the annual profits. The actual profits did not appear until the last quarter. As a trader, you have to be able to cope with that. Such a capital curve is by no means unusual.

Figure 6: Capital curve of the 4 strategies together

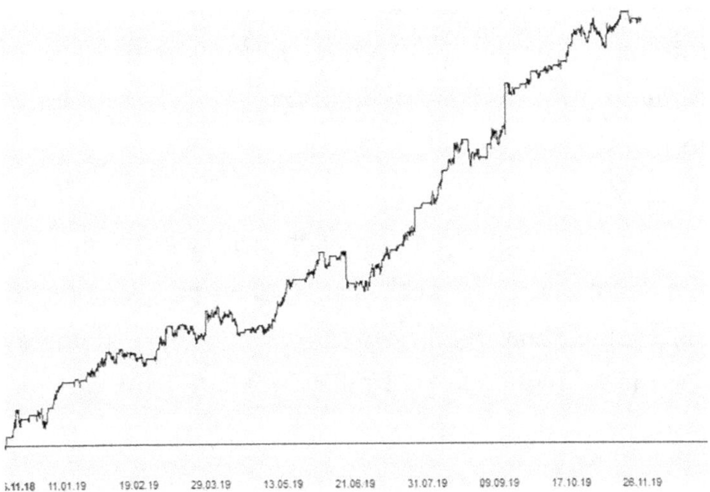

If you had traded all four strategies at the same time, you would have had a capital curve as shown in Figure 6. As you can see, there were also ups and downs, but these were easier to cope with psychologically. Moreover, the portfolio was profitable from the beginning, and the capital curve was much smoother than if you had traded only one of the four strategies, thanks to the diversification into four strategies. As a trader, I can live very well with a capital curve like this.

I would have found it much more difficult if I had had to rely on just one of the four strategies alone. The four examples are not unusual or far-fetched, and drawdowns that drag on for months occur in many trading strategies. If you, as a trader, cannot cope with them, I would recommend this kind of diversification.

That way, you will no longer be trading a particular strategy. You will start to manage a small portfolio of different strategies that produce profits and losses at different times. Of course it is important that the long-term expectation value of each strategy is positive. Therefore, before you build such a portfolio, you should take a close look at each strategy. If you have the opportunity to back-test it, then you should do so, because that way, you will at least have statistics for the system, that will tell you whether or not the expectations are positive in the long term.

3. How many strategies should you trade simultaneously?

My answer is pragmatic: not too many, but not too few either. Two strategies are clearly not enough, because with two strategies, you will not achieve the desired differentiation effect.

On the other hand, you do not need to trade twenty strategies. If you keep it between four and eight, you are on the safe side. You must also remember that you need to take a look at the performance of the individual strategies every now and then. If you act semi-automatically, or even in a completely discretionary manner, you can only trade a limited number of strategies at the same time anyway. Less is sometimes better than more, because the more strategies you trade, the more likely it is that one of them will not be profitable at all, even after a year.

4. Is it possible to diversify, even with a small account?

Of course it is. Especially in forex trading, this approach is open to traders with small accounts (under USD 1,000). Thanks to the microlots (lots of USD 1,000) you can achieve the same diversification as if you had a larger account. In fact, I find it an excellent way to familiarize yourself with forex trading and gradually build a larger account.

5. When should I start using leverage?

Once the individual strategies have been tested, and you have implemented them in your trading platform, you can start using leverage. If you are planning to trade multiple strategies, I recommend that you take a more conservative approach at the beginning. By "conservative" I mean: do not risk more than 0.1 or 0.2% of your trading capital. If you are trading minilots and you risk 20 pips per trade on a particular strategy, that is USD 20. If you only risk 0.2%, this means that you must have USD 10,000 of trading capital in order to achieve this. For example, if you only have USD 1,000, then you should trade micro lots (USD 1,000 lots). This way, you are only risking USD 2 per trade.

Things quickly become complex when you apply this type of risk management to every single strategy you trade. But that is where the advantage of a trading portfolio comes in. If the deflections on the capital curve of a single strategy and the drawdowns amount to 20% or more, then they represent only 5% of the capital curve of the entire portfolio (for example, if you trade four strategies and weight them equally). Furthermore, such losses are offset by gains in the other strategies.

Once you have gained confidence in your portfolio, after a certain period of time, and notice that your total account is growing steadily, you can start thinking about using a higher leverage.

But again: in this case, it is not a single strategy that decides whether and when you should use higher leverage, but rather, the overall portfolio and its capital curve. Only when the total account is pointing upwards should you use the leverage. That is why the following applies:

**Amateurs leverage a single strategy.
Professionals leverage a portfolio of strategies.**

Take another look at Figures 2 to 6. Which of the five capital curves would you like to apply leverage on?

I hope the reader understands what I mean here. If you look at the capital curves of the four individual strategies, you will see that you basically do not want to use too much leverage in any of these individual strategies. Only when the capital curve in the overall portfolio is smoother, should you start to use leverage, and then distribute it evenly across all four strategies.

You can think about investing less money in the weaker strategies and more money in the better strategies. But to be honest, when and how will you know which of your strategies will be "weaker" than the others? Basically, you only know afterwards. That is why I would be careful with such measures. They complicate things unnecessarily.

If one of your strategies performs so badly that it looks more like a money destruction machine, I would simply take it off the market and replace it with another. But as I said, be careful. If one of your strategies does not make any money for several months, it does not necessarily mean that it is "bad", as you will hopefully see from the examples above.

6. Forex trading is a business

All my thinking in this fourth part of the series is ultimately about looking at trading like a business.

I am sorry if I put it blandly, but: if your "activity" involves going long and short in EURUSD every day, based on some indicators, then you do not have a business. At least, that is not what I would consider a business. Because, if you were to stop going long and short in EURUSD one day, suddenly you would no longer have a "business". It is as simple as that.

Finally start trading forex, and begin to treat like a real business – a business with income and expenditure (referred to as losses), with profit margins and with an annual balance sheet. Finally, start doing this whole trading thing professionally, and stop screaming at the market like a single huckster.

This means nothing more and nothing less than that you should work less *in* your business and more *on* your business.

I know trading is exciting, even more so if you just have started. But for someone like me, who has been in this endeavor for over 19 years, in the end, only one thing matters: What has my business brought me during this fiscal year? And how can I do it even more efficiently next year?

With this book, I would like to invite you to think about whether it would not be more efficient to look at your trading business like the manager of a large fund that manages different "assets" in a risk-adjusted way.

And if you were ever planning to manage money for clients... How can you become more professional? By trading EURUSD daily based on two indicators? I do not think so...

Glossary

AUD/USD: Exchange rate between the Australian dollar and the American dollar

Bracket orders: Bracket orders help to limit losses and secure a profit by "bracketing" an order with two opposing orders. A buy order is bracketed by a sell limit order and a sell stop order. A sell order is bracketed by a buy stop order and a buy limit order

Break even: English for break-even

Broker: Financial services provider responsible for executing investors' securities orders

Cluster risk: A cluster risk arises when an investment portfolio is top-heavy with regard to certain securities, sectors, countries, currencies or asset classes

Correlation: The behavior of certain currency pairs in relation to each other. They can move either in the same direction, or in different directions, at the same time

Countertrend: Counter-movement within the main trend

Day trading: Day trading describes the short-term speculative trading of securities. Positions are opened and closed within the same trading day, with the aim of even profiting from small price fluctuations

Discretionary trading: In discretionary trading, the order is executed on the market manually, without automated trading

Drawdown: Losses that can occur, within a certain time, from the high

ECB: European Central Bank with headquarters in Frankfurt am Main

Efficient-market hypothesis: According to this theory, financial markets are efficient insofar as existing information is already priced in, and thus no market participant is able to achieve above-average profits permanently, through technical analysis, fundamental analysis, insider trading or otherwise

Expectancy: The expectations of a trading system involve a calculation that shows what the typical profit is for each trade placed. If it is negative, the strategy is not profitable. If it is positive, the strategy is profitable

EUR/CHF: Exchange rate between the euro and the Swiss franc

EUR/JPY: Exchange rate between the euro and the Japanese yen

Equity curve: An equity curve is a graphical representation of the change in value of a trading account over a certain period of time

Forex: Forex Exchange Market, international currency market

Francogeddon: On January 15, 2015, the Swiss National Bank lifted the minimum euro exchange rate of 1.20 without warning. The Swiss franc appreciated by almost 20 percent in one fell swoop

GBP/USD: Exchange rate between the British pound and the US dollar

Going long: To go long means to have bought securities, and therefore be in possession thereof

Going short: A trader is short when he sells a position without holding it (short sale).

Hit rate: The hit rate describes the ratio of winning trades to losing trades.

Leverage Effect: The use of borrowed capital can increase the return on the use of one's own capital

Limit Order: An order with a fixed price and/or time for execution

Lot: A lot is the trading unit in foreign exchange (Forex) and futures markets. In Forex, a lot in normal contracts stands for 100,000 units of the front currency (base), so in the EUR/USD currency pair, 1 lot stands for 100,000 euros.

Margin: Security retainer that an investor must deposit in order to purchase a futures contract

Microlot: One microlot is equivalent to a contract for 1,000 units of the base currency in a Forex pair

Minilot: One minilot is equivalent to a contract for 10,000 units of the base currency in a Forex pair

Momentum: Momentum informs the investor about the speed and strength of a price movement

NZD/USD: Exchange rate between the US dollar and the New Zealand dollar

OCO order (One cancels the other): A combination of stop loss and sell limit; once either the set limit or the stop price is reached, the order is executed and the other order is cancelled

Parity: Describes the point at which two currencies have the same value. The exchange rate between the two currencies is then exactly 1 to 1

Penny stocks: Shares quoted at less than one dollar

Pip: Percentage in point, smallest change in price in Forex trading.

Pivots: Support and resistance lines for intraday trading, resulting from the previous day's price movement

Portfolio: Total of all active positions of an investor

Price Action: Form of technical analysis of charts that does not use indicators

Price target: The market price that a security is to achieve, based on an analysis

Range: Sideways phase of a market

Range strategies: Strategies specifically designed to trade sideways markets

Resistance: Price level at which more sellers appear

Risk management: Comprises all measures to identify, analyze, evaluate, monitor, manage and control risks

Risk reward ratio (RRR): The RRR serves as an indicator of the usefulness of an investment. It is calculated by dividing the expected return by the maximum possible loss (stop loss)

Scalping: Trading technique where the trader tries to trade minimal movements in the market

Segregated account: Account that is kept separate from the broker's assets in the name (and ownership) of the trader

Semi-automatic trading: Trading style in which some transactions are executed manually and some automatically

Set and Forget Strategy: Method of setting stop-loss and profit targets from the outset. It is then left up to the market whether the trade makes a profit or is stopped at a loss

Stop Buy Order: Order to buy or sell securities, which is only executed when the price reaches a certain price level

Stop Loss Order: Sell order that is executed at best when a certain price is reached

Support: Price level at which buyers are increasingly active

Take Profit Order: A take profit order is used when the market reaches the desired profit price.

Timeframe: Time level of a chart display (for example, an hourly chart)

Trend Following: Trading strategy that relies on following a trend once it has been identified

USD/CAD: Exchange rate between the US dollar and the Canadian dollar

USD/CHF: Exchange rate between the US dollar and the Swiss franc

USD/JPY: Exchange rate between the US dollar and the Japanese yen

Volatility: Standard deviation. Indicates how strongly a price fluctuates

More Books by Heikin Ashi Trader

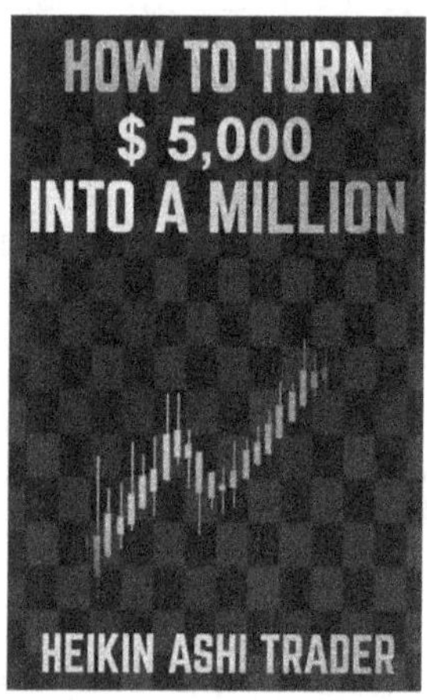

How to Turn $ 5,000 into a Million

Can you become a millionaire on the stock market? The question of how to grow a small account undoubtedly occupies every trader's mind. How do you manage to make a fortune out of a small amount? And preferably really fast?

Just as it is possible to build a real estate empire without a dollar of equity, so it is also possible to achieve high profits on the stock market with a small amount of starting capital (USD 5000 or less).

In this book, Heikin Ashi Trader presents a stock market strategy that will help the trader to succeed in this endeavor. Above all, he explains that the factor of position size plays a much more decisive role in trading success than is commonly assumed. The right question is not: how often are you right or wrong, but how big is your position if you are right?

This method is just about finding the markets where a significant movement can be expected. And once he has identified one, the trader should build a big position in that market, so that he can fully benefit from this movement.

Table of Contents

How to Trade a Range

Trade the Most Interesting Market in the World

Financial markets are predominantly trading in trendless zones, which traders call trading ranges or sideways markets. It then appears that they earn money when a market is in a trend and they should avoid trendless markets, because here there is nothing to write home about.

Despite this apparent finding, most short-term trading strategies rely on the trend-following model, although it is demonstrably difficult to implement. Most traders are more or less looking for a bigger move. The experience shows, however, that trading "moves" or "trends" is not that easy. Either the trader recognizes the trend too late, or the movement offers hardly any opportunities to enter.

There is, however, a specialized group of traders who do not care about trends. They do exactly the opposite. They trade when the market is in a range. This book describes the methods and tactics of these traders. It is not about how to identify a range and then to trade the outbreak from it, but how to trade the range itself.

Table of Contents

Trade Against the Trend!

The brokerage industry usually recommends that new traders trade with the trend. But is trading this way profitable? It is said that if you go with the trend, the likelihood that you will win is higher. Unfortunately, experience shows that most traders cannot build a profitable business this way.

Old and experienced traders used to say: You have to buy when blood flows in the streets. That means that you should act against the trend. Actually, this saying is the expression of common sense itself. The question remains: Why do traders find it so hard to put this wisdom into practice?

The new book by Heikin Ashi Trader gives ideas and tips on how to recognize such countertrend signals in the stock market, since these are usually the best trading opportunities.

Table of Contents

Part 1: The Snapback Trading Strategy

Part 2: Trading Examples

About the Author

Heikin Ashi Trader is recognized worldwide as the specialist in scalping with the Heikin Ashi chart. He has been trading this way for 19 years. He traded for a hedge fund and then went into business for himself as a trader. His scalping book "Scalping is Fun!" is an international bestseller and has been sold more than 30,000 times. You can find more information about his scalping method on his website www.heikinashitrader.net